MAX MA

Training Your Own
Service Dog

STEP BY STEP GUIDE TO AN
OBEDIENT SERVICE DOG

Introduction

Long before humans started farming, industrializing, astronomy, and all the other advancements that have led us to where we are today, man was a hunter and gatherer. As he hunted and gathered, he formed an alliance with the grey wolf (or rather, prehistoric versions of the grey wolf).

Although the grey wolf had a frightening and fearful look, many years after this alliance, the wolf started changing. Its body and temperament became less frightening, its skull, paws, and teeth shrank, its ears flopped, and to accommodate humans (who were by then providing the wolf with meat products left over after hunting), the wolf learnt many of man's complex expressions and temperaments.

Fast forward to today and the dog is "man's best friend", for good reasons. Not only are dogs good companions, over millennia of development, humans and dog have developed a simple way to understand and complement each other.

As humans have advanced, dogs have learnt to adapt to the many changes and technologies humans have invented. Today, although man has stopped hunting, dogs can still help with the process. What is interesting, however, is the fact that other than hunting and acting as security guards, as humans have evolved, so have dogs. Today, dogs wear many caps in human's society: they are show dogs, invaluable and loving companions, and helpful companions, among other things.

As you are no doubt aware, it is possible to teach a dog specific behaviors. While the most popular dog-training programs are how to train a dog as a pet (to sit, to come, to obey simple commands), in this guide we shall look at how to train a service dog.

I hope you find this book a valuable resource. Enjoy!

The information herein is offered for informational purposes solely, and is universal as so. The presentation of the information is without contract or any type of guarantee assurance.

The trademarks that are used are without any consent, and the publication of the trademark is without permission or backing by the trademark owner. All trademarks and brands within this book are for clarifying purposes only and are the owned by the owners themselves, not affiliated with this document.

Table of Contents

Understanding Service Dogs

Service dogs are assistant dogs trained to perform specific tasks and help the disabled. A service dog undergoes training to do different tasks depending on the disability. The dog assists those with various disabilities such as hearing impairment, mental illness, visual impairment, diabetes, speech impairment, posttraumatic stress disorder, seizure disorder, and mobility impairment.

Service dogs are not pets; they are working dogs because they have duties to perform. The most common breeds of dogs used as service dogs include German Shepherds, Labrador Retrievers, and Golden Retrievers.

Tasks Performed By Service Dogs

You can teach a service dog how to perform many tasks to assist you indoors and outdoors. Some of the tasks you can teach a service dog include:

1. Hearing Tasks

If you are deaf or your hearing is impaired, you can train a service dog to alert you to specific sounds. The dog cannot help you by barking because you will not hear; instead, you will train it to touch its paw, the nose nudge, or lie down next to you to alert you and then lead you to the source of the specific sound. In case of fire, it might not be safe for the dog to lead you towards the sound. Therefore, you should train the dog to only alarm you and wait for you to take necessary actions in such cases.

Some specific sounds dogs recognize at home and away from home are doorbells ringing, baby crying, phone ringing, alarm clock buzzing, vehicle honking to attract attention in garage or driveway, arrival of school or work bus, ambulance, fire truck and police car siren, smoke alarm, call from other family members, friends, or coworkers.

2. Guiding Tasks

If you are blind or visually impaired, you can train your dog to guide you thus allowing you to move around without much trouble. A guide dog will help you travel the right path, avoid oncoming traffic, locate objects such as empty seats or unoccupied areas, elevators, dropped objects, desired objects such as a spoon. You can also teach the dog to help you locate destinations such as school, hotel room, finding the exit or entrance to a room among other things.

The obstacles your dog will help you avoid and navigate through include:

* Moving objects like wheelchairs, shopping carts, people, and vehicles

* Stationary objects such as trees, buildings, pillars, stones, and parking meters

* Low hanging obstacles like tree branches and hanging clothes

* Deep potholes and open manholes.

The dog will signal you in every elevation by halting. For instance, it can halt to indicate step up into a building, descending/climbing stairs at the top/bottom of a flight of stairs, confrontation by a barrier, or warn of approach to an edge of a ditch.

3. Service Tasks

In this section, the tasks of service dogs are broad because the dogs address both daily living needs and safety or security needs.

To obtain the best services from the dog, a responsible third party will have to facilitate the interaction between you and the dog.

Some of the service tasks performed by service dogs are:

Bring the phone during an emergency

When there is an emergency such as terror, respiratory distress, or even medication side effects, a service dog will bring the emergency phone to you so you can contact a doctor or a therapist depending on the type of emergency. The emergency phone should be portable and the charger unit should be on the floor in an accessible room.

Remind you to take your prescription at set times of day

Service dogs have an internal alarm clock they will use to remind you when it is time to take your medication according to how you train the dog the different prescription times set by your doctor.

Provide you with balance assistance on stairs

If the dog is large enough, you can use him or her to climb or descend stairs by resting your hand on the withers of a large sturdy dog to steady yourself as you take each step.

Answer the doorbell

In situations where you cannot answer the doorbell and let someone into the house, perhaps due to some physical incapacity, a service dog will open the door and escort the visitor to your location.

Bring medication to mitigate symptoms

A service dog will help you when you are experiencing symptoms such as dizziness, cramps, nausea, and the fear paralysis of PTSD by bringing you the antidote medication to alleviate the symptoms.

Fetching a beverage

It is possible to train your service dog to fetch a beverage when you want or when it is time to take your medication.

Help you to rise and steady

If your dog has training in balance support work, it will keep you from falling or assist you get up after falling. The fall can be because of medicinal side effects such as dizziness and body weakness.

4. Security Tasks

Psychological injury can greatly affect your sense of security. Service dogs can offer that sense of security by offering you an innovative coping strategy, empowering you to win your measure of independence, and resist unrealistic and incorrect responses.

Some security tasks performed by service dogs include:

Aiding an escape

In case of an attack by intruders, or in case of an emergency at home, your service dog will open the front door or the emergency door for you. If your home has a storm door, you can also command the dog to move inside/outside to keep it from running off. Its reaction or behavior will help you determine if there is anyone waiting in other rooms or down the hall hence, you can escape through other doors.

Lighting up dark rooms

You can train your dog to turn on lamps or switch on lights in rooms, basements, or hallways. Well-trained service dogs can also inspect the house or even your rooms before you go to sleep. This helps reduce the fear of intruders in your home

Keeping suspicious people at bay

Well-mannered service dogs should not bark at strangers in public. However, criminals such as thieves at places like the ATM will be afraid to steal from you because they are not sure how your service dog will react.

Now that you understand the various task performed by a service dog, let us look at a systematic approach you can use to train a service dog

How To Train A Service Dog

You should give your service dog a minimum of **120 hours** of training over a period of six months. At least 30 hours of the training should be outdoors in order to prepare the dog to work in public areas obediently and unobtrusively. It is important to note that if you properly train your service dog, the dog becomes an asset.

Training your service dog starts with choosing the right dog.

Step 1: Choose The Right Dog: How To Choose A Service Dog

The success of your dog training process will highly depend on the dog you buy. Some factors to consider when choosing your service dog are:

1. The Source of Your Service Dog

Who do you want to be the ultimate source of your service dog? You can get your service dog from a rescue or breeder. Before you decide the source of your service dog, ask yourself the following questions:

How long has this rescue been in service or how long has this breeder been breeding this breed?

A breeder who has been working with German Shepherds for 20 years has much more experience than a breeder whose breeding experience is five years; having that knowledge comes from different sources. However, you should not automatically exclude new breeders/rescues but keep in mind that experience comes with practice and time.

Do you like your source?

Choosing the source of your service dog is a lot like choosing your dog's "grandparents". This person has experience with your dog's line, potential, and genetics. You need the person to be a mentor; therefore, do not opt to procure your service dog from someone whose communication you dread.

Does this source have return clients?

The best indicator of dog breeding success lies with return clients. A breeder/rescue can have good experience, but those who come back repeatedly offer the best indication of good service. If a breeder/rescuer's name constantly pops up in discussion amongst your friends, thoroughly research that breeder, and if he or she seems a perfect fit, pick your service dog from him or her.

2. The Health of The Dog

Your service dog also needs to be healthy. A healthy dog is active, has a soft, shiny coat free from dandruff, scabs, sores, or patches, and has bright eyes free of discharges.

A service dog should serve independently without needing any special attention or medication. Spend time examining the service dog you are considering buying by visiting it regularly and let the breeder/rescue produce the dog's health records and vet receipts, including the most recent vet check.

Regularly take your service dog for vaccinations and vet checks at least twice a year and weigh-ins to ensure your dog stays healthy throughout the training process.

3. Temperament

Temperament is your dog's nature, the demeanor your service dog was born with e.g. potential, confidence, self-drive, etc. You will discover a dog with good temperament if:

* The dog is willing to follow you every time you go to visit him. This shows the dog can rely on humans for directions.

* The dog has a high desire to chase and return a toy when you throw it. It indicates the dog is willing to work.

* If the dog is comfortable when you maneuver or hold him. This indicates a less fearful dog.

* The dog has good startle response. Let the dog's breeder produce sudden noise (can beat a drum) from a place where the dog cannot see him and observe the dog's reactions. An ideal dog should recover quickly and be willing to investigate the cause of the noise.

Before you buy a service dog, find out how much training the breeder has offered the dog. For example, find out if the dog knows how to sit or his/her name.

Step 2: Neuter Or Spay Your Dog

Neutering is the most common sterilization method for dogs to prevent unwanted pregnancies. All service dogs undergo neutering because males easily distract by territorial issues and females cannot work whilst in heat.

When you neuter your service dog, the dog becomes less aggressive, which is important for a service dog. Neuter or spay your dog at the age of four to six months.

Step 3: Clicker "Condition" Your Dog

Clicker conditioning is the use of the click-clack noise to mark the exact moment your dog engages in correct response and good behavior. Clicker conditioning introduces a level of precision to obedience training and skills.

To use a clicker, simply give your dog a command; when the dog obeys, click and give your service dog a free treat, 20 times in a row. For the 21st time, click and see if the dog looks for the treat. If he does not, do the click and treat exercise some more times. Your goal is to teach the dog to associate every click with a treat; hence, the dog will always look forward to the click.

Step 4: Teach Your Dog His/her Name

If your new service dog does not know his/her name, it will be difficult to communicate with the dog, get the dog's attention when you need it, or easily re-orient the dog's focus. Link your dog's name with something highly reinforcing.

Take your dog's bowl of food while it has food in it; with your service dog on a leash, stand, or sit close to him. Call your dog's name and immediately offer some of the food. Wait for the dog to look around or move away and call his name. Click when the dog looks at you and offer more food. Repeat this exercise until your service dog immediately re-orients when you call.

You can conduct this exercise 2 to 3 times a day and then gradually start using your dog's name in normal situations. Some of the correct responses you will get from your dog are immediately looking at you and moving to where you are. Every time you call your dog and he gives you the correct response, reward with a treat.

Do not use your dog's name constantly because this habit will nullify the effect of the name when you really need the dog to assist you. If you rarely use his name, he will come to realize that when you call him, it means that it is an important call and he needs to pay attention immediately. It is very important to get your dog's attention before you communicate anything to him; otherwise, the message will quickly lose its meaning.

Teaching Your Service Dog Basic Obedience Skills

Your service dog should reliably perform the following basic commands:

* Stay/sit/down

* Come on cue

* Recall

* Leave it

* Wait

The dog should also comfortably walk besides you at all times in a controlled manner. Obedience training is important because it helps you gain control over your dog.

How To Teach The "Sit" Command

Use hand signals or verbal cues as commands. Using a treat to lure your dog, hold it in front of the dog's snout, and raise it in an arc, backwards over its head. As the dog looks up to follow the treat, its bottom will drop to the floor. Click and give the treat to your dog as a reward. If your dog responds quickly and consistently to the command, add the command word "sit".

How To Teach The "Come" Command

Commence teaching the recall skill indoors or in an enclosed back yard away from other animals because your dog will not manage to recall if distracted. Call the dog; once the dog comes, click, repeat the cue word "come" and reward. If the dog does not come, do not rebuke the dog because this will make the dog more reluctant to come to you the next time you call.

Another thing you can do to reinforce the recall skill is to pay attention and watch for that moment when your dog will start running towards you on his/her own volition. The moment you see your dog coming towards you, say the cue word "come".

Although it was the dog's idea to come to you, you will get the credit for the whole thing by giving your dog a command and rewarding it. Anytime your service dog does something on his own and you give him a treat, he will do the action repeatedly with pleasure.

Some don'ts that will affect the reliability of your dog's recall skills are:

* Do not call your dog without reason because eventually, your dog will end up ignoring you. Whenever you call your dog and he/she obeys, give a treat.

* Do not call your dog for punishment. If you do, the next time you call him, he might not obey because he is afraid that you will punish him.

* Do not call your dog when you are angry.

* Do not call your dog if you are going to put him in a crate or lock him in a room and leave.

Teaching Your Dog How To Behave When Leashed

Leashing your service dog is not an option; it is a law. You have to leash your service dog to ensure those who live around you are safe from possible attacks by your dog. Start leash training your dog indoors.

With a leash attached to your dog's collar, take him for a walk. When the dog reaches the end of the leash, turn and move in the opposite direction. If the dog comes back to your side, click, and give a treat. Repeat this exercise until you notice your dog watching you; do not forget to reward your dog after every correct response.

Encourage your service dog to catch up with you by using the word "hurry, hurry". Once your dog masters the indoors, you can now move from indoors to outdoors and try this exercise.

When you are in public and your service dog's focus wavers, turn and walk in the opposite direction until your dog moves back to your side. In this way, your dog will learn that he can only goes to places if he walks nicely.

Distractions are good learning opportunities. Add them to your training process.

Teaching Your Service Dog Not To Greet Other People

This is a very important step in your training process. Your service dog has to focus on you and not anyone else. You might need instant help; if your service dog is busy running around to greet other people, it will not be of any assistance to you. To train your dog this step, you need a friend or a family member.

With the dog sitting next to you and looking at you, let them (a friend or a family member) approach you slowly. If the dog turns to look at the approaching person, they (a friend or a family member) should immediately stop and ignore the dog. Once the dog's focus returns to you, click and treat the dog.

Continue doing this exercise a few more times and eventually, the dog will learn that paying attention to the approaching stranger earns him no reward; hence he will pay attention to you. Also, teach your service dog not to take food from the ground, pay attention to strangers talking to him, or pay attention to immobile vehicles at the garage and driveway.

The relationship between you and your dog is very important; the attention you get from your dog highly depends on how you handle the dog. Spend time with the dog and allow the dog time to be alone. Take your service dog for silent walks, brush your dog's head, or back with your hand to make the dog feel good, and allow the dog to stretch.

Respect your dog for the dog he is and never nag your service dog. If you do all this, you will create a very strong unbreakable bond between you and your service dog.

Teaching Your Dog To Quietly Lie Down For Long Periods

One of the important behaviors you should teach your dog is settling quietly for long periods and minding his own business. To teach your dog this behavior, you can use a tether.

A tether is a four feet steel cable with a snap on both sides. One end snaps to your dog's collar and the other end can snap to a stationary object. To teach your dog this behavior:

1. Take your service dog to a safe, visible spot and attach one snap of a tether to his collar and the other to a stationary object. The tether should be at least 30 inches long to permit movement.

2. Remain positive and calm because your reaction will determine your dog's reaction.

3. Allow your service dog time to realize he is on a line. Lightly hold the tether and slowly move away from him as you release your hold.

4. Moving away from him will make him want to rush towards you, causing a jolt against the tether.

5. Your service dog will start struggling because he has realized he cannot be with you. Keep calm and do not talk to him until he stops struggling.

6. Allow the dog time to keep quiet and relax. Return to him 30 seconds after he is quiet, click, give praise and a treat.

7. Repeat this exercise every day and as your service dog learns how to relax on tether, slowly increase the time you tether him.

8. Include the command word "lay", click when he obeys, and reward.

A tether will allow your service dog to discover comfortable lying positions. When you tether train your service dog, he will know what to do when you present him with a mat or a leash and will settle peacefully for the period you want him to.

Teaching Your Dog How To Be Confident

You can have a smart, intelligent, and calm service dog, but if the dog is not confident, he will not perform his tasks in situations where confidence is a necessity. One of the most important things you can do for your service dog is to build a strong sense of confidence in him. There are two kinds of confidence:

1. The genetic make-up of your service dog: In the choosing your service dog step, this is the confidence you were looking at. Many kind and calm dogs cannot think or go out on their own. Unfortunately, you cannot change the genetic makeup of a dog.

2. Confidence built by success: You have control over this type of confidence. Start by challenging your service dog to go beyond his comfort level and every time he succeeds, reward him with a treat and praise. Your dog will feel confident after he has succeeded in a training step and will want to repeat the act to please you.

To build your service dog's confidence, practice the following:

1. Bring your service dog with you whenever you can as a way of introducing the dog to many places and people.

2. Lift your service dog onto a tree and when he feels steady on his feet, use a cue word to ask the dog to take a few steps. Click and reward. Repeat this exercise until your service dog can jump up all by himself and walk along the trunk of the tree.

3. Go for hikes off leash in safe and private places, letting your service dog be a dog.

4. Go for rides in the car often.

5. Expose your dog to other friendly animals as often as you can.

6. Take trips with your service dog and let him explore different environments.

Repeat these exercises until your dog matures and you will have a very confident service dogs.

It is important to point out that if you lack confidence, you cannot train your service dog to be confident. Confidence is not about achieving perfection; confidence is a state of mind that enables you to do something. If you worry about getting the whole thing wrong, not looking right, or not being able to control your service dog in public access, this will create a state of un-sureness and timidity for you and your service dog.

Have positive conscious thoughts and deliberate positive actions at all times; this will help you succeed in your service dog training process.

How To Teach Your Dog Its Work /Specialized Skills

The skills you teach your service dog depend on your disability. Define the purpose of your service dog (the tasks he is going to help you perform).

Create a list of the tasks you want to teach your service dog and plan how you will approach every task. Some of the special skills training include:

How To Teach Your Service Dog Mobility Disorder Skills

If you have a mobility disorder, you can teach your service dog how to retrieve objects, press switches, and lamps, offer you support, close, and open doors. Retrieving objects task include:

* Locating and recognizing objects

* Picking up the objects

* Giving you the objects

To teach your dog how to locate and recognize an object, place an object such as a phone at a place where your dog can clearly see it. When your dog approaches the item, use the command word "phone", click and give him a treat. Repeat this exercise several times. You will notice your service dog becomes proactive about approaching the phone. Every time he approaches it, click and give a treat.

After your dog has learned how to locate an object, train him how to pick it up. Place the object in the dog's mouth and use the command word "hold". Click when your dog holds the object and reward. Repeat this regularly until your dog can hold the object on command.

Place the object a short distance away and using the command words "phone" and "hold", let the dog locate the object and pick it up; use your recall word to call back the dog while he is still holding the object. Do not forget to click and reward your service dog after every correct step.

After bringing the object to you, let your dog sit and drop the object. Use the cue word "give" as he drops the object, click and give a reward. Repeat these steps twice a day and always keep the sessions short (5 to 10 minutes) so your dog does not get bored

How To Teach Your Service Dog Guiding Skills

If you are visually impaired, you cannot train your service dog on your own; you need assistance from a professional trainer, a family member, or a friend. Some of the skills you will train your service dog are going around obstacles, stopping/giving you a signal at elevation changes, walking in a straight line, and stopping at any curb.

To teach your service dog this skill, you first need to teach your service dog how to walk in a straight line. With the help of an assistant, walk with your service dog on a straight path and let the dog keep your pace. The dog should be on you left hand side and just ahead of you.

Use command words and leash correction to communicate to your dog. Repeat this exercise until your service dog learns how to guide you in a straight line. Reward your dog every time he does this correctly.

Now introduce an obstacle such as walls or chairs into your training. Let your service dog guide you toward an obstacle. When you get near the obstacle, let your assistant command the dog to turn away from the obstacle. This step will require practice and patience for the dog to learn and choose the best direction to take.

Train your dog to refuse obeying commands that may lead you into danger such as incoming vehicles or walking into potholes by using the command word "stop". Let your assistant give the command when you are near danger and when your dog stops, praise him, and give him a treat.

Choose a sound or a place "nudge point" that your dog will use to signal you at elevation changes. Do not go to crowded places like malls until your dog learns how to lead you independently.

How To Teach Your Service Dog Hearing Skills

If you are hearing impaired, the tasks you will teach your service dog include reacting to household sounds like an alarm clock, a phone ringing, among other things. You also need to teach your dog how to respond to different sounds like smoke alarms, doorbell rings, how to lead you to them, and how to react to a sound that indicates danger.

For this, you need to teach your service dog sign language in order to communicate with him. Before you give your service dog any sign command, make sure he is directly looking at you. Sign and touch your nose with a finger to give your dog the "watch me" sign/ command. When your dog makes eye contact, give him an open flash of your hand (instead of clicking) and then reward him. Repeat this exercise two or three times a day.

Introduce the other command signs you want to teach your service dog, lure him into a place with high value treat, give him an open flash of your hand or a thumbs up sign when he does the sign you are teaching him and then give a treat.

Start by teaching your dog alert skills. How do you want your dog to let you know of an alarming sound? Add a "nudge point"– a nudge point is the place where you want your dog to touch you when he is alerting you. Point to the "nudge point" and using the command sign "touch", let him nudge the place. Give him an open flash of your hand and reward.

Add distance and specific sounds after your dog learns the "nudge point". Remove the command sign "touch" and focus on the specific alarming sounds. Every time your service dog nudges you, give him an open flash of your hand and reward. Change your position, your dog's position, and add distance and the source of the specific sound.

Once your dog has mastered every alarming sound and its sign, teach him how to lead you to the source of the sound and how to connect the two (alerting and leading). This training requires practice and patience. You also need an assistant to help you in activities like activating an alarm sound and giving commands.

How To Teach A Service Dog Autism Service Dog Skills

If you suffer from autism or other sensory processing disorders, you cannot train your service dog. However, with the help of an assistant, you can train your service dog how to help you relieve anxiety, depression, and self-harming behaviors.

Use a technique called deep pressure therapy (DPT) to make attacks of any sort shorter and easier to bear. DPT is generally pressure to your chest, abdomen, or any other body part accessible to your dog. A small sized service dog can lie on your chest and a large sized dog can drape his paws across your lap and then press his head into your torso to provide pressure.

To teach these skills, get some treats and find a couch. Place the treat in front of your dog's snout and slowly move the treat toward the back of the couch. Pat the couch and say you dog's name. If your dog puts his paws up, use the command word "paws up", praise, and give him the treat.

If your service dog is small, wait until all the four paws are up before you command "paws up". You will also need a treat to get the dog into a "down" command on the couch. Practice this exercise until when you command "paws up", your service dog can repeat without a treat.

Now lie on the couch and pat your chest or abdomen and command "paws up". You may have to use a treat to lure the service dog because he will likely be confused. Repeat this until your dog understands the skill you aim to teach.

If your service dog is small, he should lie on your chest vertically with paws on your shoulders and head next to yours, but if he is large, he should place his paws on either side of your hips with his chest horizontally across your lap. Call your dog off your chest by saying, "paws off".

Increase the time your dog is required to lie on your chest and replace the treats with verbal praise.

Teaching Your Service Dog When He Is Off Duty

It is good to allow your service dog to play, and have some time alone. You can use a cue word to tell your dog when he is off duty. To do this, invite a friend to your home and let him bring along a dog toy. When your service dog looks at that person's direction, use the cue word "play", click, and reward. This will signal to the dog that it is OK to approach the person. Repeat this action once or twice a week.

How To Teach Your Service Dog Public Access Manners

You should train your service dog how to behave well and have good manners in public. Some dos of public access you should teach your service dog are:

1. Walk nicely on a leash without lagging, forging, circling, or pulling (unless the dog's task requires tension on the leash). When your dog attempts to pull, lag, or circle, do the following:

* Slide your hand closer to the collar.

* Keep the leash loose between your hand and the collar.

* Use an effective snap or a pop motion with the leash and release.

* Give one correction at a time and do not give verbal correction.

* If your service dog does not stop pulling/circle, correct again with a stronger snap.

Repeat the above until you have your dog's attention and he stops trying to pull/circle. Every time your dog reacts to your snap, click and give a treat.

2. Ignore all distractions such as other dogs. Start by slowly approaching a distraction that your service dog can handle and let him observe the distraction from a distance: Do not approach the distraction until your service dog relaxes.

Practice "calming sits" from a distance and when you are in close proximity to the distraction and your service dog cannot move away, let him stay down beside you when you are standing still.

Concentrate on your service dog, enforce the stay, and do not allow him to change position. Release him with a different command and praise him or give him a treat when he obeys. This will teach him that he does not have to pay attention to other things because they earn him no treat.

Repeat this exercise several times with the presence of a distraction.

3. Remain quiet at all times unless performing specific tasks you have taught him. Your service dog should not bark, growl, grumble, or whine.

When your service dog gets excited and starts making noises, correct him using the leash collar correction. Use a command word such as "quiet" or "keep calm" to help him regain control. Click and give him a reward when he is quiet.

If your service dog barks at you when you correct him, escalate your correction to ensure he realizes the seriousness of his misconduct; when your service dog growls, grumbles, barks, or whines for no good reason, correct using the command word "quiet." Click and reward for the correct reaction

4. Train your dog to keep his nose to himself at all times. Do not let your dog go sniffing at objects, people, and even food.

Sense of smell is one of a dog's strongest senses; if your service dog goes sniffing at objects or people, he will not concentrate on his work. This will also imply to other people in the public that your dog is bad mannered.

When you see your service dog trying to sniff at objects both indoors and outdoors, use the command word "stop" and when he stop his actions, click and give a reward. Repeat this action every time you see him trying to sniff at objects or food until this behavior stops.

5. Your service dog should urinate and defecate only on command. Housetrain your dog before taking him to public places. If your service dog is young, outings should be short enough to avoid public "accidents". Your service dog cannot be a service dog if it goes urinating or defecating inappropriately.

How To Train Your Service Dog To Relieve On Command

Choose a relieving area you can use each time you take your dog outside for bowel relief. Using a familiar area will stimulate your dog relief reflexes. Choosing a concrete or gravel relieving area can be helpful in teaching your service dog to relieve on hard surfaces.

Take your service dog to his relieving area. The goal of this step is to have your service dog walk by your side in a controlled manner to the relieving area. Once you are at his relieving area, use the command word "OK", allow him to sniff the ground and walk in a circular pattern, and do not allow him to move to fresh ground. If he is reluctant to move, take two steps forward immediately followed by two steps backwards to encourage him to move.

Wait until your service dog is urinating or defecating before saying, "go potty". This will help your dog relate what you are saying to what he is doing. Once your dog learns to relate, modify your timing to teach him to relieve on command.

Use the command while he is circling or showing other signs to indicate he is preparing to relieve.

Finally, begin giving the command as soon as he reaches his relieving area.

Your service dog should perform the tasks you have taught him: it is not an option. He should do pertinent tasks to mitigate your disability. Also, as the owner and trainer of your service dog, it is your responsibility to make sure your service dog remains well-groomed and clean at all times.

Service Dog Certification

After you teach your service dog all the skills he needs to know and the tasks you want him to perform, you have to certify him so he becomes officially recognized. By certifying your service dog, the dog will have access to places where other dogs such as pets do not have access.

Research the governing body for particular type of service dog such as guide service dog. To certify your service dog, you require the following:

1. Vaccine confirmation documents

2. Documents to prove you need a service dog and a recommendation letter from a doctor explaining your disability as well, as how a service dog can ease your life/disability.

3. Vet check document to confirm your dog's good health and good character.

After getting the above documents, send them to the appropriate licensing body and wait for your application to be processed.

And then you have a certified service dog!

Conclusion

It is important to mention that service dog training is a continuous process that requires planning every step of the way. Be thorough as you teach your dog, be patient, and do not move to another behavior before your service dog understands one behavior.

Finally, if you enjoyed this book, would you be kind enough to leave a review book on Amazon?

Thank you and good luck!

Made in the USA
San Bernardino, CA
15 March 2017